THE TWELVE DAYS OF SUMMER

written by
ELIZABETH LEE O'DONNELL
illustrated by
KAREN LEE SCHMIDT

MORROW JUNIOR BOOKS
NEW YORK

For Joe E.'s father
E. L. O.

For little Marie
K. L. S.

Printed in Singapore at Tien Wah Press. 1991.
1 2 3 4 5 6 7 8 9 10
Library of Congress Cataloging-in-Publication Data
O'Donnell. Elizabeth Lee
The twelve days of summer / Elizabeth Lee O'Donnell.
p.   cm.
Summary: A cumulative counting verse in which a girl enumerates
what she sees at the beach. from one little purple sea anemone to
twelve gulls-a-gliding.
ISBN 0-688-08202-5—ISBN 0-688-08203-3 (lib. bdg.)
1. Counting—Juvenile poetry.   2. Beaches—Juvenile poetry.
3. Marine fauna—Juvenile poetry.   [1. Beaches—Poetry.   2. Marine
animals—Poetry.   3. American poetry.   4. Counting.]   I. Title.
PS3565.D55T9 1990
811'.54—dc20
[E]   89-35161 CIP   AC

On the first day of summer,
I saw down by the sea
A little purple sea anemone.

On the second day of summer,
I saw down by the sea
Two pelicans
And a little purple sea anemone.

On the third day of summer,
I saw down by the sea
Three jellyfish,
Two pelicans,
And a little purple sea anemone.

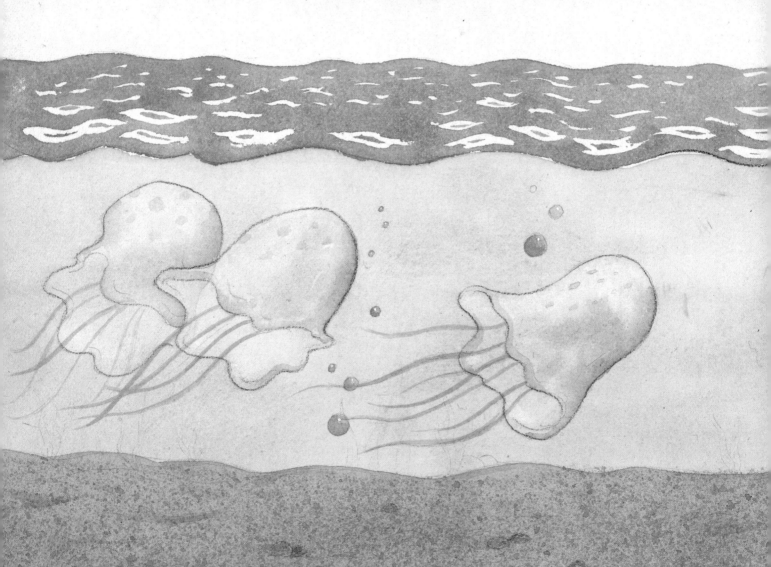

On the fourth day of summer,
I saw down by the sea
Four 'pipers running,

Three jellyfish,
Two pelicans,
And a little purple sea anemone.

On the fifth day of summer,
I saw down by the sea
Five flying fish,
Four 'pipers running,
Three jellyfish,
Two pelicans,
And a little purple sea anemone.

On the sixth day of summer,
I saw down by the sea
Six squid a-swimming,
Five flying fish,

Four 'pipers running,
Three jellyfish,
Two pelicans,
And a little purple sea anemone.

On the seventh day of summer,
I saw down by the sea
Seven starfish strutting,
Six squid a-swimming,
Five flying fish,
Four 'pipers running,
Three jellyfish,
Two pelicans,
And a little purple
sea anemone.

On the eighth day of summer,
I saw down by the sea
Eight crabs a-scuttling,
Seven starfish strutting,
Six squid a-swimming,

Five flying fish,
Four 'pipers running,
Three jellyfish,
Two pelicans,
And a little purple sea anemone.

On the ninth day of summer,
I saw down by the sea
Nine seals a-barking,
Eight crabs a-scuttling,
Seven starfish strutting,
Six squid a-swimming,
Five flying fish,

Four 'pipers running,
Three jellyfish,
Two pelicans,
And a little purple
sea anemone.

On the tenth day of summer,
I saw down by the sea
Ten dolphins playing,
Nine seals a-barking,
Eight crabs a-scuttling,
Seven starfish strutting,
Six squid a-swimming,
Five flying fish,
Four 'pipers running,
Three jellyfish,
Two pelicans,
And a little purple
sea anemone.

On the eleventh day of summer,
I saw down by the sea
Eleven waves a-crashing,
Ten dolphins playing,
Nine seals a-barking,
Eight crabs a-scuttling,

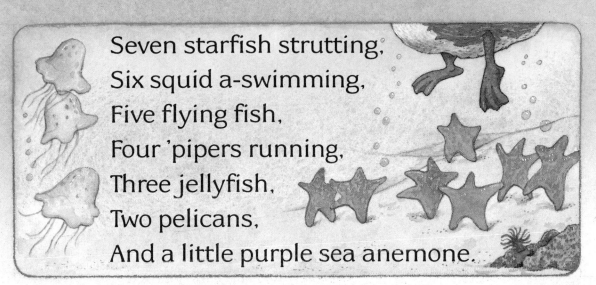

Seven starfish strutting,
Six squid a-swimming,
Five flying fish,
Four 'pipers running,
Three jellyfish,
Two pelicans,
And a little purple sea anemone.

On the twelfth day of summer,
I saw down by the sea
Twelve gulls a-gliding,
Eleven waves a-crashing,
Ten dolphins playing,
Nine seals a-barking,
Eight crabs a-scuttling,
Seven starfish strutting,
Six squid a-swimming,
Five flying fish,
Four 'pipers running,
Three jellyfish,
Two pelicans…

And a little purple sea anemone.